# A New True Book

# THE CROW

### By Ruth Hagman

CHILDRENS PRESS ®

CHICAGO

Crow moccasins embroidered
with glass beads

PHOTO CREDITS

The Bettmann Archive—6, (2 photos), 11
(right), 13 (top left), 32, 33 (2 photos), 35

© Reinhard Brucker—© Field Museum, Chicago,
2, 13 (bottom left, top, center & bottom right), 16
(right), 17 (left), 18 (2 photos)

© Michael Crummett—4 (2 photos), 7 (right), 14
(right), 16 (left), 22 (center & right), 24 (right),
26 (2 photos), 28, 37 (right), 39 (left & center),
41 (4 photos), 42 (2 photos), 44, 45 (top,
center, bottom left & bottom right)

H. Armstrong Roberts—© Camerique, 11 (left)

Historical Pictures Service, Chicago—8, 9, 30

North Wind Picture Archives—24 (left)

© Rob Outlaw—37 (left)

© Chris Roberts—17 (right), 22 (left)

Root Resources—© Mary A. Root, 7 (left)

© John Running—Cover, 14 (left), 39 (right), 45
(top right)

UPI/Bettmann Newsphotos—15, 21

Chuck Hills—map, 4

Cover: Crow Fair

Library of Congress Cataloging-in-Publication Data

Hagman, Ruth.
    The Crow / by Ruth Hagman.
        p.    cm. — (A New true book)
    Includes index.
    Summary: Discusses the history, traditional lifestyle,
language, world view, and contemporary life of the
Crow Indians.
    IBSN 0-516-01103-0
    1. Crow Indians—Juvenile literature. [1.  Crow
Indians.  2.  Indians of North America—Great Plains.]
I.  Title.
E99.C92H34   1990                    90-37679
978'.004975—dc20                     CIP
                                     AC

# TABLE OF CONTENTS

The Crow decorated their horses' trappings and their other possessions with beautiful beaded designs (left). A Crow elder wears an eagle-feather warbonnet (below).

# CROW COUNTRY

About five hundred years ago, the Crow were part of a group of Native Americans called the Hidatsa. In the 1300s, the Hidatsa and the Crow traveled south from Lake Winnipeg in Canada into the Devil's Lake country of North Dakota. In the late 1500s, the Crow broke away from the Hidatsa, who were farmers. The Crow became buffalo, or bison, hunters. They followed the buffalo

Chief Pretty Eagle

Chief Bear Claw

herds. For many years, they
lived near the Black Hills
of South Dakota.

In the early 1600s, the
Crow headed west into the
Yellowstone River Basin of
Wyoming. Later, they settled
in the Bighorn Mountains

6

Left: The Yellowstone River. Right: Billings, Montana.
Land of the Crow reservation is in the background.

and along the Tongue, Powder, and Yellowstone rivers of Montana.

For many years this territory was their home. In the late 1800s, the United States government forced the Crow onto a reservation. Today they live near Billings in southeastern Montana.

7

# THE HORSE AND THE BUFFALO

Coronado traveled north from Mexico looking for fabled cities of gold.

In 1540, the Spanish explorer Francisco Vásquez de Coronado brought horses to what is now the southwestern United States. Horse trading slowly spread from there to the northern plains. By 1740, the Crow were trading beaver furs and buffalo robes for horses.

Before Native Americans had

horses, buffalo hunting was much harder. The whole tribe went on a hunt and took everything they owned with them. They used travois pulled by dogs to carry their belongings. Travois were made of two trailing poles with a platform between

Horses could pull much larger travois than dogs could, and the loads could be heavier.

them. The dogs were small
and pulled loads of less than
twenty pounds. They liked to
play and chase rabbits.
Often the travois were
broken. Food, clothes, and
tipi poles were scattered
everywhere.

Horses helped the Indians
travel farther and faster.
Hunting trips were shorter
and more efficient. On
horseback, the hunters
would find and circle a
buffalo herd and shoot the

Today, buffalo live in Yellowstone Park (left). Hunters on horseback brought down the buffalo (right).

animals with their arrows. With horses, they were able to kill large numbers of buffalo on a single hunt.

The buffalo gave the Crow food, fuel, clothing, and shelter. Buffalo meat was

pounded and dried to make
pemmican, a mixture of
meat, berries, and fat. The
kidneys, heart, brain, and liver
of the buffalo were also eaten.

The hide, or skin, was
made into soft leather for
clothing. It was also made
into rawhide. With rawhide,
the Crow made cooking
pots, tools, weapons, and
moccasin soles. Hides with
the hair left on were treated
to make buffalo robes, which
were used for blankets.

A wooden bowl (top right) and carrying case. Buffalo products included rawhide drums (left), horn spoons (below), and moccasins (bottom left). Bottom right: Crow beadwork

CROW

CROW

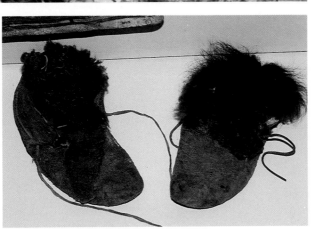

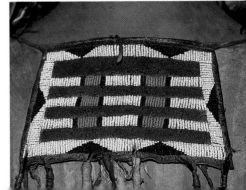

Today the tipis at the Crow Fair are made with canvas covers.

Tanned buffalo hides were used to make tipi covers. Muscle tendon, or sinew, was used like thread for sewing. Dried buffalo droppings, called chips, were burned in campfires.

14

# WORK AND CRAFTS

Crow men and women
had separate tasks. The
women built the tipis.
They peeled the bark from
several slender lodgepole-
pine logs. Then they made a
cone-shaped framework of
pine poles and tied the

Crow women processed the buffalo hides
and dried strips of the meat in the sun.

poles together near the top.
They scraped the hair from buffalo hides, tanned them, and sewed them together to make a tipi cover. After the men painted it, the cover was placed on the wooden frame, and the tipi was ready to live in.

The Crow were an artistic

The dress (left) is covered with elk teeth and is worn with a beaded belt. The necklace (right) is made of beads and beaver teeth.

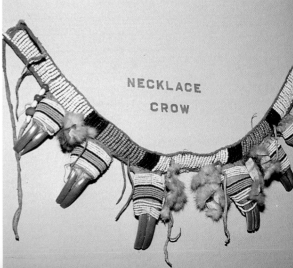

A Crow boy's outfit (left).
Two Crow men in eagle-feather
warbonnets (right).

people. In their spare time
they made jewelry from deer
hooves, elk teeth, and bear
claws. The men used the
feathers of golden eagles to
make headdresses called
warbonnets. The women
embroidered clothing and

17

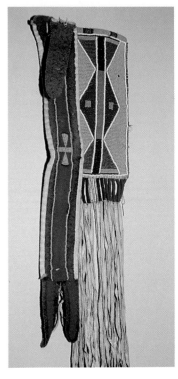

A folding rawhide parfleche decorated with geometric designs (left). A beaded bag (right)

moccasins with porcupine quills and glass beads. Both men and women painted designs on rawhide parfleches, folding bags used to store belongings. The women made geometric designs on boxes. The men painted realistically. They drew animals, people, and natural objects like the sun on their drums, shields, and robes. They drew picture stories about their hunting and raiding adventures.

The artists made their paint from brown, red, and yellow clay. Sometimes they burned animal bones and wood to make charcoal. They mixed the charcoal with fat to make the color black.

# FAMILY LIFE

The Crow had matrilineal families. This means that they traced their descent through the mother's ancestors. The children belonged to the mother's clan.

Before the 1900s, there were thirteen Crow clans. They had names like Whistling Water or Sore-Lip Lodge. The clans were scattered around the

Crow family eating

countryside, but they
banded together for wars,
celebrations, or hunts.

The Crow had small
families and were kind to
their children. Crow
children learned to work

A Crow mother and son
(above) cool off in
the Little Bighorn
River. Crow boy (right)
and girl (left)
wear traditional clothing
at the Crow Fair.

by helping their parents.
The Crow loved to play games.
Playing games made the
children strong and prepared
them for adult life. The
adults liked to sing songs
and tell stories. In this way,
the children learned about
their history and traditions.

# LANGUAGE

The language of the Crow expresses their feelings, beliefs, and traditions. Their jokes, stories, songs, and legends tell us how they feel about their world and about themselves.

When the Crow wanted to speak with people who didn't know their language, they used simple hand gestures that were understood by everyone.

A Crow and a scout (left) communicate by sign language.
Women (right) "say" the Lord's Prayer in sign language.

This sign language let them
"talk" to white men and
people from other tribes.

They also used smoke
signals to alert their tribe
when enemies or buffalo
were nearby. They made
long and short puffs of

smoke by fanning a blanket over a smoldering campfire. These smoke messages could be seen from far away.

In the late 1800s, the United States government tried to wipe out Crow culture. They thought they could make the children forget their old way of life if they put them into year-round boarding schools. They wanted to "take the Indian out of the children" and make them like the white people. The teachers were told by the government to make the children speak English. Fortunately, the plan failed. Today the Crow language is spoken by 80 percent of the tribe, and the Crow children still learn the old traditions and beliefs.

A Crow grade-school pupil displays her artwork (left). A junior-high boy studies American history (right).

# SPIRITS AND SUN DANCING

The Crow believed that
everything in nature had a
spirit—mountains, rocks,
plants, and animals. The
grizzly bear, elk, and
golden eagle were powerful
animal spirits. The Crow
thought of themselves as
part of the natural world.
The animals were like
brothers and sisters. When
the Crow needed help, they

called upon the spirits.

When they wanted to find buffalo or win a battle, the Crow held a Sun Dance. First, they cut and trimmed a tall tree for the Sun Dance pole. The men who were to take

Crow men built a "sweat lodge" like this one in which to take a steam bath before the Sun Dance.

part in the Sun Dance
took a bath in the steam
made by pouring cold water
on hot rocks. Then the
medicine man made slits in
the chest of each man
and put long wooden pins
through the slits. The pins
were attached to rawhide
ropes that were tied to the
top of the Sun Dance pole.

Several Plains tribes besides the Crow held the Sun Dance.

The man would pull against
the ropes, trying to break
free. He would ask the sun
spirit to send him some
of its energy and make
him strong.

# WARFARE

All Crow boys wanted to become great war chiefs. Chiefs like Bell-Rock or Plenty Coups were honored and respected.

When Crow men talked about their enemies—the Blackfeet, Cheyenne, and Sioux—they told war stories. The children liked to hear about war deeds. During a raid or surprise attack, the men often did not try to kill the enemy. Instead, they

A mounted Crow man "counting coup" on a fallen enemy

touched him with a "coup stick." The children learned that "counting coup," touching an enemy with a coup stick and getting away, was braver than killing him. Stealing an enemy's weapons and horses and leading a victorious war party were other brave deeds. When the boys became teenagers, they were ready to fight in real battles. The years spent learning to shoot bows, ride horses, and hunt buffalo made them strong and brave.

Portraits of strong and proud Crow men

# CROW HOMELANDS DISAPPEAR

At first, the Crow were friendly with the white explorers, prospectors, pioneers, soldiers, and trappers who came to their country. A treaty of friendship was signed with the United States government in 1825.

But life changed for the Crow when white people started to hunt the buffalo. White hunters killed entire

White hunters killed millions of buffalo for their hides.
By 1900, there were only about 500 buffalo left alive.

herds for their skins and
tongues and left the rest of
the meat to rot. Without
the buffalo, the Crow
people were starving.

   In the late 1800s, the
Crow tried to fight off their
Northern Cheyenne and

Sioux enemies, but diseases brought by the white people had killed many Crow and left the tribe weak. They had to ask the United States government for help. In return for the help, the government took land that the Fort Laramie Treaty of 1868 had said belonged to the Crow. The government sold the land to white farmers, ranchers, and miners. By 1900, the U.S. government had forced the Crow onto a reservation.

# BATTLE OF THE BIGHORN RIVER

The Bighorn River and the land around it in Montana are part of the Crow reservation. White people came onto the Crow reservation to fish and hunt. In 1973, the tribe decided they had to protect their economic interest in the

The Bighorn River flows through Bighorn Canyon.

river's wildlife. They closed
the river to white sportsmen.
This started the Battle of the
Bighorn River.

The state of Montana said
the Crow couldn't keep the
white people off their land.
But the Crow felt that
treaties gave them control
over the Bighorn River.

The Bighorn battle went
on for seven years. In 1981,
the U.S. Supreme Court ruled
against the tribe. A 52-mile
stretch of the river was given
to Montana. Now the Montana

A sign along the Bighorn River (left) marks the reservation boundary. Some Crow are cattle ranchers (center). Coal mining on Crow lands (right)

Department of Fish, Wildlife, and Parks governs the river. The Crow people wonder if the loss of the Bighorn River means that the government will try to take more of their reservation land. The Crow feel the U.S. government ignores treaty rights.

# LIFE TODAY

Today, about eight thousand tribal members live on the Crow reservation in southeastern Montana. The tribe has its own constitution. Both men and women make political decisions.

More than half of the people on the reservation are unemployed. Some people have government jobs as custodians, miners, nurses, or park aides. The Crow receive some money

Bill Yellowtail (bottom right) and Angela Russell (top right) are Crow members of the Montana state legislature. Janine Pease Windy Boy (top left) is president of Little Bighorn College. Robert Yellowtail (bottom left) was a respected Crow elder.

from leasing mineral rights (coal, oil, natural gas) and farmland.

Crow children learn about
their language and traditions
in schools on the reservation.

In 1869, Chief Plenty
Coups told his people,
"Education is your most
powerful weapon. With
education you are the white
man's equal; without
education you are his
victim."

42

The Crow remembered
Plenty Coups' words. In
1985, Little Bighorn College
was opened. The Crow
people are proud that their
language is still spoken.
Today, their own people
teach the Crow children
about their heritage, and
their traditions are still
strong.

A cultural event—the
Crow Fair Powwow and
Rodeo—is held each

Native Americans camp out in tipis at the Crow Fair.

summer. People from all
around the world come to
share the singing, dancing,
and feasting. For five days,
people of many races and
from other tribes unite
with the Crow in a bond of
peace and friendship.

Powwow visitors meet old
friends, make new friends,
and take home many memories.

# WORDS YOU SHOULD KNOW

**artistic** (ar • TIS • tik) — having the ability to draw and paint and create pleasing designs

**buffalo** (BUHF • uh • loh) — a large mammal like a cow with a big head and a hump on its back; also called a bison

**charcoal** (CHAR • kohl) — partially burned, blackened wood or bones

**clan** (KLAN) — a group of related families descended from a common ancestor

**constitution** (kahn • stih • TOO • shun) — a set of rules or laws for the government of a group of people

**coup** (KOO) — a quick, bold, and clever move

**economic** (eck • ih • NAH • mik) — having to do with making a living

**efficient** (ih • FISH • uhnt) — able to do something with the least waste of effort or materials

**embroider** (em • BROY • der) — to sew designs on a material with different colored threads or beads

**geometric** (gee • oh • MET • rik) — shaped like squares, circles, or triangles

**gesture** (JES • cher) — a movement of a part of the body

**Hidatsa** (hih • DAHT • sah) — a Native American tribe that lived in farming villages along the Missouri River

**legend** (LEH • jind) — a story from the past

**matrilineal** (mat • rih • LIN • ee • yal) — descended through the mother; tracing family descent through women

**mineral rights** (MIN • er • il  RITES) — rights to the use or sale of minerals such as coal or oil found on a piece of land that may be owned by someone else

**moccasin** (MAHK • uh • sin) — a soft leather shoe made without a heel

**parfleche** (par • FLESH) — a folding pouch made of rawhide, used for storing food or belongings

**pemmican** (PEM • ih • kin) — a high-energy food made from dried and shredded meat, berries, and fat

**prospector** (PRAH • spek • ter) — a person who searches for deposits of ore, such as gold or copper

**quill** (KWILL) — a stiff, sharp spine that sticks out of the body of a porcupine; the stiff shaft of a bird's feather

**rawhide** (RAW • hyd) — an untanned animal skin with the hair removed

**reservation** (rez • er • VAY • shun) — a piece of land kept as a home for a Native American tribe

**sinew** (SIN • yoo) — a tough fiber cord that fastens a muscle to a bone

**smoldering** (SMOHL • der • ing) — burning with a low flame and giving off a lot of smoke

**tan** (TAN) — to treat an animal skin to make it soft and flexible; to make leather out of hides

**territory** (TAIR • ih • tor • ee) — an area of land that a group of people regards as their own

**tradition** (truh • DISH • un) — an old custom

**travois** (trah • VWAH) — a device for carrying loads, made of two poles that trail on the ground with a net or platform between them

**treaty** (TREE • tee) — a written agreement between two groups, having to do with trade, peace, land rights, etc.

**warbonnet** (WOR • bahn • it) — a headdress consisting of a band around the forehead decorated with upright eagle feathers

# INDEX

## About the Author

*Ruth Hagman has written for adults as well as children. This is her first book for Childrens Press.*